Window Cleaning Hustle

Easily make $1000 or more a month cleaning windows part-time

by Shawn Lemond

1.Introduction

In this book, I will give the information you need to begin a part-time window cleaning hustle. You also could also grow your business into a full-time gig if you play your cards right!

Window cleaning is a great business to get into that requires very little overhead to get started. It also can be quite lucrative. It is not unusual for a window cleaner to make anywhere from $50-$100 an hour.

The great thing about window cleaning is there are windows everywhere that need to be washed. Just about every store and home in your city or

This book is an entry-level book on how to start cleaning windows. Everyone needs to start out somewhere but often are lost on where to begin.

Here is something you need to understand, you will not be able to know everything you need to know about window cleaning by reading one book or watching one video.

I believe this book is a great outline of what to do to start making $1,000 a month. I recommend doing more research because there is a lot to learn that many pros throughout the years have learned.

The good news is that right now there is sufficient information and resources especially online to get started and on the right track quickly.

There will be lot of question marks when you first decide to go about a window cleaning business. This book was created to give you some direction and enlightenment.

2. Some Necessities

Equipment

BARE MINIMUM
-Small and Large Squeegee
-Small and Large Brush
-Bucket
-Extra Squeegee Replacement Rubbers
-Extension Pole
-Huck or Microfiber Towels
-Dish soap(such as Dawn). I like to mix Dawn soap with some Windex.

This site has just about every out there for window cleaning in one place. I like it because the prices are about as low as you can get. They also offer free shipping on orders over $100.

Remember that to start out you only need the basics. This site has so much that you might get carried away with buying too much to start with!
You can always get more products as you grow in your business.

I also use Amazon as well. Amazon will have a few things here and there for window cleaning, often at good prices. You might want to price check a few things between these two sites.

Uniform

It is a pretty good idea to get a uniform created for your business. This is so you can show up to present your services and at job sites in a professional manner.

You don't NEED a uniform, but it helps.

If you are just starting out and aren't confident yet 100% of your abilities, that is ok.Showing up in a clean uniform with your business logo will give you more respect.

 A potential client will not have an idea of how experienced or large your cleaning company is. By wearing uniform things often will be easier, and you will feel better about presenting your services.

When I first started, I was thinking in my mind, these people have no clue that I don't even have hardly any jobs yet!

Showing up and acting professionally and well dressed, helped me get over that hurdle. I went out like I had done it a million times before, and presented myself well.

A Note on Tools and Supplies

If you are going to be doing larger jobs or homes, you will need to have more equipment than what I listed earlier. As you grow and start doing more complex jobs, you will see that it will help to learn more about different types of equipment and supplies that can be used.

One thing I learned is that there are quite a few things that are good to have that aren't exactly necessary. I bought a state of the art squeegee and brush that I thought would be cool to have. I actually went back to using my cheaper set of tools, because it just worked better for me.

There are times I could use the state of the art tools, but if you are on a budget you could pass on it. So be aware of that.

If you are going to be doing residential homes, you will need some booties that will go on your shoes when you enter the house. That is a necessity for that job.

You also will need a ladder that can go up to the second story, if you are planning to clean on the second story, and can't do it via extension pole.

Some things will be needed as you take on certain types of jobs, and there will be no way around it. So be prepared to spend more as you grow and develop.

Office Space

When you are first starting out you will want to create a space for both your paperwork and marketing materials. You also need a space to house your equipment.

Even if you only have an apartment/house and not an actual office/storage space, this will work.

When you are first starting your needs will be limited. As you grow, you will get better at creating a space for your business. In this way, you can always find and work on what you need to do.

Your Vehicle

If your starting small just about any type of vehicle will do. All you need to make sure of is that your basic equipment is able to fit.

The best case scenario is that you have either a truck or van that can fit all that you need very easily, such as a ladder.

Many window cleaners advertise or wrap their cars with their logo and phone number/information. This is great because any time you drive around town, you are getting free advertising.

Your vehicle is important because the better it looks, drives, and stores relevant equipment the better. It's no coincidence that the big time window cleaners usually have awesome professional vehicles.

If your not quite there yet or aren't planning to spend a lot, do the best you can in getting your vehicle set up decently.

3. How to Clean Windows

Practice

You're going to want to get some major practice in if you are beginning to clean windows. If you already have professional experience that will be a plus. You might not so plan to spend quite a few hours practicing your window cleaning skills.

Even if you have to practice on one or a few windows over and over, it will be a great help. You will need to learn how to properly brush, squeegee, use an extension pole, and wipe tracks and sills.

Professional window cleaners that have been cleaning for years can go quickly, with good technique. At the same time keeping mistakes to a minimum.

Go to YouTube to learn some skills. Especially basic videos teaching you how to window clean. You won't be a pro at first but with practice, you will get decent.

It might take you even a couple months to get really good, but if you can do a decent job within a few weeks, it should be ok to start.

Watch some Youtube videos on different types of windows being washed, and how each window cleaner handles the job.

If you are going to start doing residential windows this will be a bit hard. Search out how to clean screens, window tracks and many other different tips on residential window cleaning on YouTube.

YouTube

I am 100% convinced that you MUST check out window cleaning videos on YouTube and you are a newbie. Unless you are getting on the job training already, or have experience, I believe it is a must.

I will already give you an outline of what to do to start a window cleaning hustle in this book. Getting an outline is the hard part.

Now that you have it you will want to search Youtube for Videos to fill in the gaps on the information you need to focus more on:

Check out Youtube Videos on:

-Window Cleaning Techniques (brushing, squeegee, pole work)
-Some examples of different building and homes being cleaned
-Types of equipment
-Advertising Ideas
-Pitfalls and don't do's!
-Just about any other kind of video that will teach you new things you don't know

There are quite a few window cleaners on YouTube that are sharing this information for free. You may want to just try to get the basic information for newbies though at first.

Don't be overwhelmed or intimidated if they begin to discuss stuff that is way over your head (water fed pole, high rise cleaning, etc.). You don't need every type of equipment right away. Even the best pros didn't start out knowing everything.

I know of a millionaire who owns a window cleaning company. He still uses a lot of old-school type equipment and does not have every new gadget out there.

This is why window cleaning is so awesome. What kind of service business could you learn how to do on YouTube!

4. Types of Window Cleaning Jobs

Window Cleaning Storefronts

Storefronts are some of the easiest types of windows to get into cleaning. It is pretty easy to go into a storefront and ask for someone in charge. They should will be able to tell you YES or NO when you ask them if you can clean their windows.

There are different types of storefronts. Some are small mom and pop stores. Some are more well known but the manager or person on site has the option of letting you clean the windows.

Some storefronts are well-known corporations who beat around the bush and will not really answer your question. It will seem that talking to the right person about doing the job is impossible. Even if you get an answer on who to talk to, it still feels like you just can't get your foot in the door.

I believe that approaching storefronts is the best way to being window cleaning. There are more than enough out there that have the potential to say yes to your services.

For the most part, you will get from $10-20 smaller, $25-35 medium, $40-50 large, storefront. If you really need the work you usually will have to shoot low. Often $10-$20 per storefront will get you more jobs. Just don't sell yourself too short. You should be making at least $40-50 an hour at the lowest.

Canvassing

An important method to get jobs is to drop off business cards or flyers to businesses in your area. I get the best response doing this in person.

I will show up in my uniform and ask to talk to the manager/owner. If not them, then anyone that can give the go ahead to clean the windows. Give them a quick quote.

 I will let them know that their windows are dirty
(if they are) and if they have anyone that cleans their windows.

I find this method works best.

There are other ways to let them know about window cleaning, but doing it in person will put them on the spot. If you can talk them into it, you can clean the windows right on the spot.

People have other things on their agenda, you need to get straight to the point.

If you can get a price and date set for the first cleaning, that would be awesome!

Rejection

When approaching strangers for window cleaning jobs, you will get rejected. You will get rejected more than you probably am comfortable with I suppose.

Many will be courteous, but will not be interested. Some will seem like they are interested, but will not commit. Be sure that you get your pitch down right and hit as many potential customers you can.

If you continue to make good pitches to customers consistently, you should begin to secure some jobs.

Salesmanship

If you are trying to get window cleaning jobs you need to be a good salesman. Yes, you are cleaning windows, but you must be able to convince people to let you do it.

The good news is one you get down your pitch and understand
What will lead people to say yes, you will be ok.

Have a clear idea of what you are going to say to introduce yourself and what you could do for them (clean their windows).

Also, there will be objections or at times just a bewilderment as if they had never heard of wind cleaning before! You must have some ideas on how to answer these in order to get them to say yes.

Some common objections are:

-price is too much
-already have someone doing it
-we don't really need it
-we clean it ourselves

Objections disguised as almost commitments:

-sounds like a great idea! we will get back to you
-probably, I'll let you know

Most of the time these are the objections you will get. If you are able to convince them that having their windows washed on a scheduled basis is necessary or important that would be good.

Even if they seem like they might call you, often they won't. Many times they are just being polite, which is cool but won't earn you money.

Try to get them to commit to having their windows washed on the spot or next day, even if it takes a first time cleaning discount 25-50% off (up to you exactly).

Once in a while, you will find a prospect that gets excited and seemed like they were just waiting for a window cleaner to come along. These are the people that you want to get a scheduled cleaning done right away!

Then after you clean them to make sure that they know you can do it on a scheduled basis immediately.

I guess you could say some prospects are cold, warm, or hot to the idea of window cleaning.

The best idea is to focus on those that are the most likely to be hot or even warm and hone in on them. Those that are very cool to the idea most likely aren't interested no matter what.

These are usually those who are in low-income residential/business locations or they really don't give a rip if their windows are clean or not.

The thing to understand is that cleaning windows isn't rocket science for you or for the client. It can be done quickly and the customer can quickly understand what you are trying to do. If you can just convince them to have you clean at least once (hopefully scheduled), that is major.

Window Cleaning Route

The thing you will want to shoot for is signing up customers for consistent cleaning. Always ask the customer if they would like to have their spot cleaned on a scheduled basis. You can offer them weekly/bi-weekly, monthly/every two months, or quarterly cleaning etc.

This will work out great because if you are able to get a client at $50 a month. In one year you will receive $600 for a yearly cleaning from just one customer ($50 X 12 months in a year).

If that spot takes an hour to clean each time...

You will make:
$600=12 hours work during the year. Not bad at all.

Once you start getting quite a few customers on a scheduled basis you can create routes where you will go from job to job, to job
on scheduled days and start raking in cash.

You will need to start having a schedule book as well as a list of clients, and dates you will be cleaning.

Residential Jobs

Residential jobs are a niche that can be lucrative.

Although it is lucrative, it can be harder. The reason being is that each home can be way different. You will need a lot more options and tools than most small commercial jobs. Each mistake or problem will be magnified because the homeowner will be right there watching.

Most window cleaners charge well over $100 for a home to be cleaned. Some larger homes can be over $500.

Screens, Frames

If you are going to clean homes start learning to clean window screens and frames really well. I would advise you to practice at your own home or buddies, before taking a real job. There is nothing worse then taking a residential job and having no clue what to do, or breaking something.

Small Buildings

If you are just getting started, I believe the hardest job you may try to take is a small building. This type of job is great because it may be an office building with quite a few windows to clean. It may have a second story in which you could clean via extension pole.

It will be larger than most jobs, so the amount you could get in pay can be really good. Especially if they require monthly/quarterly cleaning.

Mid Level and High Rise

I won't discuss anything much about large mid level and high rise buildings. These types of jobs aren't really for beginners. They will usually require thousands of dollars in equipment and proper levels of experience.

5. Getting Paid

Pricing Window Cleaning Jobs

Window cleaning pricing can be interesting. If you are just starting, there is a tendency to not charge as much. This is okay, but make sure that you are making $40-$50 an hour at LEAST. This is the bare minimum.

I would also advise you to get a copy of THE WINDOW CLEANING BUSINESS and/or STRAIGHT TALK ABOUT WINDOW CLEANING BIDDING. Both of these books are by John Baxter. You will learn a ton about bidding and pricing window cleaning.

Invoices and Receipt Book

Get an invoice book and receipt book. Use an invoice to bill your customer. Have your receipt book ready to give a receipt for each payment.

They may want to pay later via check in the mail. Give them an address to mail all check payments to.

Another option is that you can use paypal to send them an invoice via email. They then can pay you online. It is pretty easy once you learn how to do.

Taking Credit Card Payments

Taking credit card payments is an option even if you haven't done it before. I actually had a company send me a free card reader that attaches to my phone. I then got the company app that allows me to take payments.

Everything is free, although you must pay them a small percentage to process your card payments which is normal.

Two of the most popular companies that help you take payments on your phone are Square and Paypal.

6. Marketing

Your Business Name and Logo

An important part of your business is your business name and logo. Even if you are doing windows on a small scale, it still is great to get an actual business name and logo. You can get a logo created on Fiverr for a couple bucks or just about any other freelance site that has graphic designers.

Customers will be much more inclined to speak to you if you already look and present yourself like you know what you are doing. A great business name and logo (on a uniform or business card) will help.

I won't tell you what to name your business but try to do a good job! You might want to research what others have named their window cleaning business.This will help you get a feel for how to find a name. Make sure you are not using a name someone already else has!

Online Presence

Ok, so you are excited to clean windows and want to be seen as a legit window cleaner. You should find a way to get an online presence. This basically means that if people are searching for window cleaners in your area, they can find your business.

You will be able to sign up to do this for FREE when you first start. I wouldn't say you need to pay a lot of money for this or any at all. I would in most cases say that you should not pay any money on this at first.

The window cleaning companies that are the most relevant and well known in your area are already getting jobs and they are easily found online in your city/area.

This is because they often have many good reviews on the web, and have been around a lot longer online. They also may already have made enough money to put some funds into online ads and marketing, which has boosted their presence online further.

You want to basically get IN the game when it comes to being found online.

This is so you can begin to get to more people on the internet in your area. You can also now be found online so if someone hears about you they can look you up and see what you are all about. At that point you may want to have some business hours, information, pictures, reviews, posted online.

Also remember that even when you haven't done one job yet, You can still present your business the way you want it to be seen. So do all you can to present your business as legit and awesome, even if you are new.

A good idea is to check out different companies online and see what they are already doing (why reinvent the wheel) that is working.

If you are capable you can create an online presence yourself. Or if needed with a bit of help from some freelancers. The cost should be a couple bucks here and there.

Yelp

Yelp is a great site that gives information on the top businesses in your area. They usually start with the best and well know for each business category. If someone looks up WINDOW CLEANER in your city, there should be a top ten (or so) list, with many more listed down the line.

You can list your business on Yelp then put some pictures and basic information. If someone wants to, they can review your services. Reviews are VERY VERY important on Yelp. If you have a lot of good reviews, it can lead to a ton of business. Yelp is a must have for any business in your area.

Google

Get your business registered on Google. This is important because this is the most popular search engine.

Google now has GOOGLE BUSINESS. This is where you register your business with Google and your business will be findable with your information on google. You also can create a free basic website for your company with Google business. This is great if you are not ready to set up an official site for your business.

Website

You can get a website up for your business, but this will cost you money each month. It can be a benefit, but you must decide if you are going to do it right away or later. The one drawback is the cost.

Facebook

Setting up a Facebook business page is easy. I think it is really relevant because it is easily shareable with others and you can add lots of pictures, fun information, and videos. You also can share with others via online advertising using Facebook ads.

Instagram

Instagram is pretty cool to have in your arsenal of online advertising. You can use it to post content, get followers, and even interact with some. I'm still skeptical that it would bring you much business, but it couldn't hurt.

Don't spend too much time here though if it is a distraction. Creating window cleaning posts seems fun, but remember that you are trying to clean windows and not become an internet marketer.

Craigslist

Craigslist is a great place to get customers for window cleaning. As you read this book, I am not sure if Craigslist will continue to create ads for free.At some point, I heard Craigslist was going to begin to charge a fee for businesses to post ads.

In the past, I created many window cleaning ads on Craigslist for free with good success. Especially when I first started. You just list the service you do and whatever other relevant information you want.

Remember you are trying to convince them to call you to do a good job. You can also add pictures.

Other Options

There are other sites and platforms you can try to advertise on. I'm guessing that there are about a handful of other sites that might get you some results in your area. It can't hurt to try them out if they are free to use.

Business Cards

After you get a logo created you can use it on your business card. You can either have a freelance designer create the card design for a couple bucks, or create your own design.

Do the best you can to make it professional. It wouldn't hurt to look online for some examples of other window cleaning business cards.

I usually use a site online like Vistaprint to print out a couple hundred cards at a low price.

Cold Calling

I have used this technique and it can work. If you are calling different organizations, companies, or businesses ask them if they are interested in window cleaning. You can email them information, mail it, or drop it off in person if they are wanting services.

Flyers, Postcards, Leaflets

These are awesome tools to put in peoples hands. These can give a lot more information to the customer than just a business card. I like to hand these out along with my business card at times.

You can get hundreds of these and get them into the hands of prospects however you like. Give basic information on your business, contact information, and the service you provide.

Be sure to check online, for inspiration. I would go to google and type in WINDOW CLEANING FLYER OR WINDOW CLEANING AD. Then I would click IMAGES.

Check out some ideas you may like. Note and jot it down and then you can then turn this into your own flyer or ad that you get printed cheaply.

These are very important if you are just starting out because it gives you a point of contact and something to present to your customers that's official. You can leave this to people and they can call you if interested.

Door Hangers

These can be put on the doors of homes or businesses. Many window cleaners go into richer neighborhoods and put door hangers on expensive homes. This is very smart because the wealthy have more income to pay for a window cleaning service. Not everyone is interested in window cleaning because they often don't think about spending money on it.

Door hangers can cost way more to print as well than just small leaflets or flyers. So being selective on the demographics you give it too can be smart.

Let's just say it costs $100 to get about 750 door hangers printed. This is doable. If you just two people want the service you will make some good money. If no one wants the service you will be out $100.

So it might be worth it or might not. If you are comfortable trying this early great. If not find another advertising method for the time being.

Referrals

Once you do a job for a customer, it would be great to have them refer others. You can give them a few business card or flyers to share. You also could encourage them to share about your window cleaning service on social media. Every bit of advertising helps!

Direct Mail

If you have a group of people you would like to reach out to, you could do it by direct mail. The post office can give you a discount rate if you want to mass postcard potential customers through the mail. You will have to pay quite a bit, but it is an option if you think it may work.

Email

Using email is a great way to contact people to ask if they need window cleaning.

The good thing is that you can do it from home or wherever you are. You also will be able to send over materials in pdf form such as flyers or documents that a potential customer can see. It is great to have a ton of tools available.

This is a good idea to get ahold of some people you would not be easily able to approach in person. Someone of higher authority may be more willing to talk to you via email than in person sometimes.

Online Ads

You can create pay-per-click ads online as well. This is when you pay a social media site or other companies money to post ads that customers can click on.

The good news is that you can target online people who you think are interested in window cleaning. They can just click your ad and will be given a chance to check out your offer or information.

The bad news is that you will have to pay a fee every time someone clicks on your ad. It can be quite expensive if you don't know what you are doing.

It also can be a good idea if you can find a way to make it work and pull in clients.

Follow Up

It is always good to follow up with those potential customers who:

-got their windows cleaned once before
-those that you may have talked with before and did not decide to commit.

Even if they did not pull the trigger last time, they may be more likely when approached again. If they showed some interest in the past it is a good sign.

Competition

An important thing to do is check out the competition in your area. You might want to check out the window cleaners nearest to you that work in your immediate vicinity. You might want to see how they relate and present themselves to customers online.

A good idea is to check out a few that fall in line with what you plan to do and take some notes.

The funny thing is once you decide to start a window cleaning business, you might begin to spot some window cleaners out and about doing jobs.

It does not hurt to check them out and see what they are doing. Both the jobs and the equipment they are using. You might find it pretty interesting.

You probably won't be able to get to the more experienced level right away. You are focusing on the easier jobs in most cases. This means although you might be making less money, many of the jobs you take will be fast and quick. So don't compare yourself to others too much, you are just getting started blazing your own path.

Becoming a Specialist 3-4 Main Services

A good idea is to find out what times of window cleaning services you are good at. You also can find out what types of jobs really work for you and you enjoy doing. If you can find a particular niche you really like you can become an expert in that area. You can get a higher amount of satisfied customers and referrals as well.

I love doing storefronts. The reason being is that they are quick and I can create a route that works for me. Think of 3-4 main types of service you would like to focus on. It is good to become a master at a few things, than mediocre on a ton.

7. Upsells and Additional Services

You can always add other services along with window cleaning. Services such as pressure washing, gutter and ceiling fan cleaning, all are services additional services that could be offered.

Although you are advertised as a window cleaning company, you may want to inquire with customers later and let them know you can do these types of services as well.

8. Don't Forget

Insurance

Having insurance for your company is a great idea. Some people/managers will want to see proof of insurance (although not all). This is especially true when dealing with larger jobs or buildings.

Safety Issues

An important issue in window cleaning is safety. You must keep your safety, as well as the public's a priority at all times. Don't put yourself or others at risk. Don't try to clean windows that you are not capable of cleaning. If you don't have the tools for the job walk away. On some jobs you will be able to do 95% of the windows, some will not be accessible.

Let the customer know you can't do those, and do only what you can do safely.

Some common issues:

-Since you are using water and soap to clean, always make sure you wipe and do not leave water on the floor. You don't want others to slip.

-When using an extension pole be aware at all times if someone is near. Also, do not use the pole in a way that could put others at risk.

-If climbing a ladder use caution and learn to do it right. If you are going to the second story, be aware you are taking a risk.

-If you are scraping debris off a window with a scraper be careful. You could cut yourself or scratch a window.

There are other issues as well, so be aware and be safe.